HAMSTERS

by Sophie Geister-Jones

Cody Koala

An Imprint of Pop!

popbooksonline.com

abdobooks.com

Published by Pop!, a division of ABDO, PO Box 398166, Minneapolis, Minnesota 55439. Copyright © 2020 by POP, LLC. International copyrights reserved in all countries. No part of this book may be reproduced in any form without written permission from the publisher. Pop!™ is a trademark and logo of POP, LLC.

Printed in the United States of America, North Mankato, Minnesota

102019
012020

THIS BOOK CONTAINS
RECYCLED MATERIALS

Cover Photo: iStockphoto
Interior Photos: iStockphoto, 1, 5 (bottom left), 5 (bottom right), 7, 11 (top), 12, 15, 16–17, 19, 20; Shutterstock Images, 5 (top), 9, 11 (bottom left), 11 (bottom right), 13

Editor: Meg Gaertner
Series Designer: Sophie Geister-Jones

Library of Congress Control Number: 2019942765

Publisher's Cataloging-in-Publication Data

Names: Geister-Jones, Sophie, author
Title: Hamsters / by Sophie Geister-Jones
Description: Minneapolis, Minnesota : Pop!, 2020 | Series: Pets | Includes online resources and index.
Identifiers: ISBN 9781532165719 (lib. bdg.) | ISBN 9781532167034 (ebook)
Subjects: LCSH: Hamsters--Juvenile literature. | Hamsters as pets--Juvenile literature. | Rodents as pets--Juvenile literature. | Pets--Juvenile literature.
Classification: DDC 636.9356--dc23

Hello! My name is
Cody Koala

Pop open this book and you'll find QR codes like this one, loaded with information, so you can learn even more!

Scan this code* and others like it while you read, or visit the website below to make this book pop.

popbooksonline.com/hamsters

*Scanning QR codes requires a web-enabled smart device with a QR code reader app and a camera.

Table of Contents

Chapter 1

Behavior

Hamsters are **nocturnal**.
They sleep during the day,
and they are awake all night.
They play in their cages then.
Hamsters can be noisy when
they play.

Watch a video here!

Hamsters **hoard** food. They fill their cheeks with food. Then they hide it somewhere in their cage. Hamsters are **territorial**. They should be kept alone. They will fight other hamsters.

Hamsters have four front toes and five back toes.

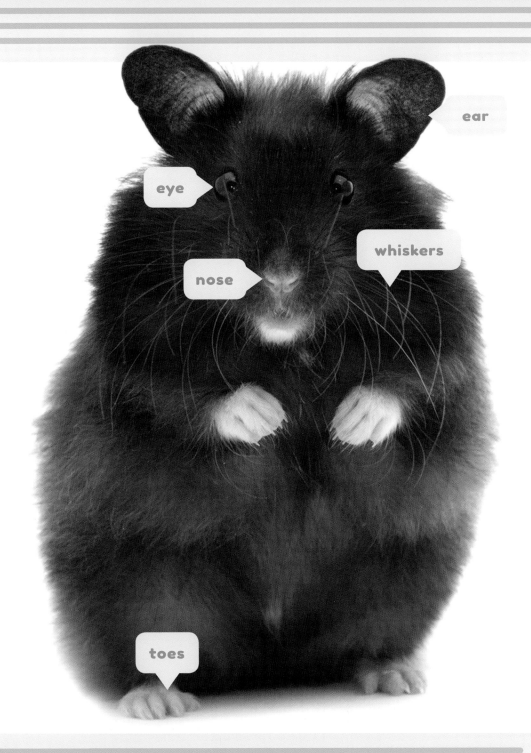

History

In 1930, a man found many golden hamsters in a field. He brought them home. He raised the babies. Since then, people have been keeping hamsters as pets.

Learn more here!

Many Types of Hamsters

There are more than 20 **species** of hamsters. Each species looks and acts different. Many only live in the wild. Five species make good pets.

Learn more here!

Golden hamsters are one
species. They make good
pets. Golden hamsters can
have short or long hair.

Dwarf hamsters are another species. They are very small.

Hamsters cannot see well. They depend on their senses of smell and hearing instead.

Chapter 4

Hamster Care

Hamsters live in large cages. The cage floor should have a layer of bedding. The best bedding is made from paper or wood chips. Cages should be cleaned weekly.

Complete an activity here!

bedding

Hamsters have a lot of energy. A running wheel gives them a place to run. Cardboard tubes and small boxes are also good toys. Hamsters can climb on them or hide in them.

Hamsters drink water. Hamster food can be bought at a pet store. Hamsters should also have toys to chew. Chewing keeps hamsters' teeth healthy.

A hamster's teeth are always growing.

water bottle

Owners can play with their hamsters. Owners should hold their hamsters **gently**. Hamsters that are treated gently are often friendlier. Hamsters can be good **companions**.

Making Connections

Text-to-Self

Do you know someone who has a pet hamster?
What color is it?

Text-to-Text

Have you read other books about hamsters?
What did you learn?

Text-to-World

Not all hamster species make good pets. What
qualities make an animal a good pet?

Glossary

companion – a person or animal that is friendly and spends time with another person or animal.

gently – in a soft or kind way.

hoard – to collect many things and guard them.

nocturnal – active at night.

species – a group of animals of the same kind that can have babies together.

territorial – not good at sharing a space or thing with others.

Index

Online Resources

popbooksonline.com

Thanks for reading this Cody Koala book!

Scan this code* and others like it in this book, or visit the website below to make this book pop!

popbooksonline.com/hamsters

*Scanning QR codes requires a web-enabled smart device with a QR code reader app and a camera.